GRAPHIC HISTORY

JOHN BROWN'S RAID ON HARPERS FERRY

by Jason Glaser
illustrated by Al Milgrom,
Bill Anderson, and Charles Barnett III

Consultant:
James M. McPherson
Professor of History
Princeton University
Princeton, New Jersey

Capstone press
Mankato, Minnesota

Graphic Library is published by Capstone Press,
151 Good Counsel Drive, P.O. Box 669, Mankato, Minnesota 56002.
www.capstonepress.com

Printed in the United States of America

1 2 3 4 5 6 10 09 08 07 06 05

Library of Congress Cataloging-in-Publication Data
Glaser, Jason.
John Brown's raid on Harpers Ferry / by Jason Glaser; illustrated by Al Milgrom, Bill Anderson and Charles Barnett III.
p. cm.—(Graphic library. Graphic history)
Summary: "In graphic novel format, tells the story of John Brown's 1859 raid on Harpers Ferry, Virginia"—Provided by publisher.
Includes bibliographical references and index.
ISBN 0-7368-4369-8 (hardcover)
1. Harpers Ferry (W. Va.)—History—John Brown's Raid, 1859—Juvenile literature. 2. Brown, John, 1800-1859—Juvenile literature. I. Milgrom, Al, ill. II. Anderson, Bill, 1963– ill. III. Barnett, Charles, III, ill. IV. Title. V. Series.
E451.G57 2006
973.7'116—dc22 2004029083

Art and Editorial Direction
Jason Knudson and Blake A. Hoena

Designers
Jason Knudson and Jennifer Bergstrom

Colorist
Benjamin Hunzeker

Editor
Christine Peterson

Editor's note: Direct quotations from primary sources are indicated by a yellow background.

Direct quotations appear on the following pages:
Page 6, from *To Purge This Land With Blood, A Biography of John Brown,* by Stephen B. Oates (New York: Harper & Row, 1970).
Page 11, from *Life and Times of Frederick Douglass*, by Frederick Douglass (Secaucus, N.J.: Citadel Press, 1983).
Pages 13, 15, 18, from *A Voice From Harpers Ferry, 1859,* by Osborne P. Anderson (New York: World View Forum, 2000).
Page 24, from original interview text published in the *New York Herald* on October 21, 1859, as reprinted in *John Brown, 1800-1859, a Biography Fifty Years After,* by Oswald Garrison Villard (Boston, New York: Houghton Mifflin, 1910).
Page 25, from John Brown's original note at the Chicago Historical Society (http://www.chicagohs.or

TABLE OF CONTENTS

CHAPTER 1

A NATION DIVIDED

Brown and his family joined others who were against slavery. They were called abolitionists. Brown's father, Owen, was very religious.
Can you tell me what this Bible passage means?
All people are our brothers and sisters.
BIBLE
Brown's family secretly helped slaves become free. They were part of the Underground Railroad. This network of people helped slaves escape to Canada.
You may hide here until it is safe to travel.
With your help, we will soon be free.

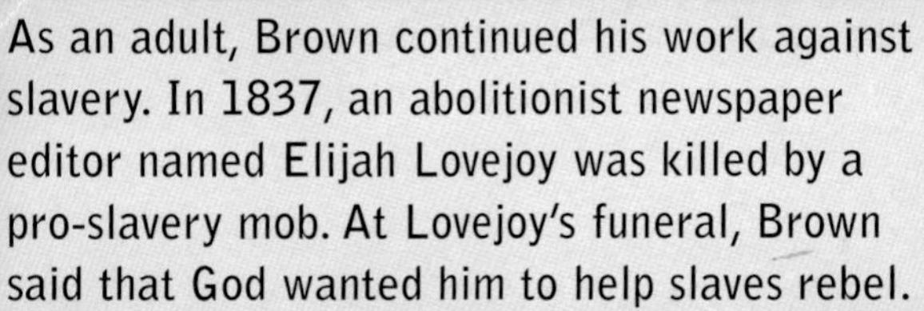

When Brown was 50, the U.S. governmen passed the Fugitive Slave Act. That law let slave owners capture any black people they claimed were runaway slaves.

In 1855, Brown joined his sons who were fighting to keep the U.S. territory of Kansas free from slavery. At that time, territories voted on whether to have slavery or not. A group of raiders called Border Ruffians forced people to make slavery legal in Kansas.
If violence is what it takes to fight slavery, then I will join the fight.
Brown became the leader of a group of soldiers from Osawatomie Creek in Kansas. They chased many pro-slavery raiders out of Kansas.
For Kansas!
For freedom!
For John Brown!

In 1856, some Border Ruffians burned the city of Lawrence, Kansas. The small town was against slavery.
These Ruffians must be punished. I will kill them for this outrage.
That May, Brown and his sons killed five raiders. Brown was then wanted for murder.
They say the men were found with their heads cut off! Did you do this?
I killed no innocent man.

Brown had to leave Kansas. He decided to fight slavery in a new place. Brown grew a long beard to change his appearance. During the next two years, Brown met with abolitionists in the East and North.
I need more weapons to continue my fight.
We shall give you money and 200 Sharps rifles.
I will use them to attack Harpers Ferry.
Harpers Ferry was a military outpost on the border between Maryland and Virginia. Thousands of military weapons were made and stored in the federal arsenal and armory there.
I will take the town's weapons and give them to the slaves. Then they can fight for their own freedom.

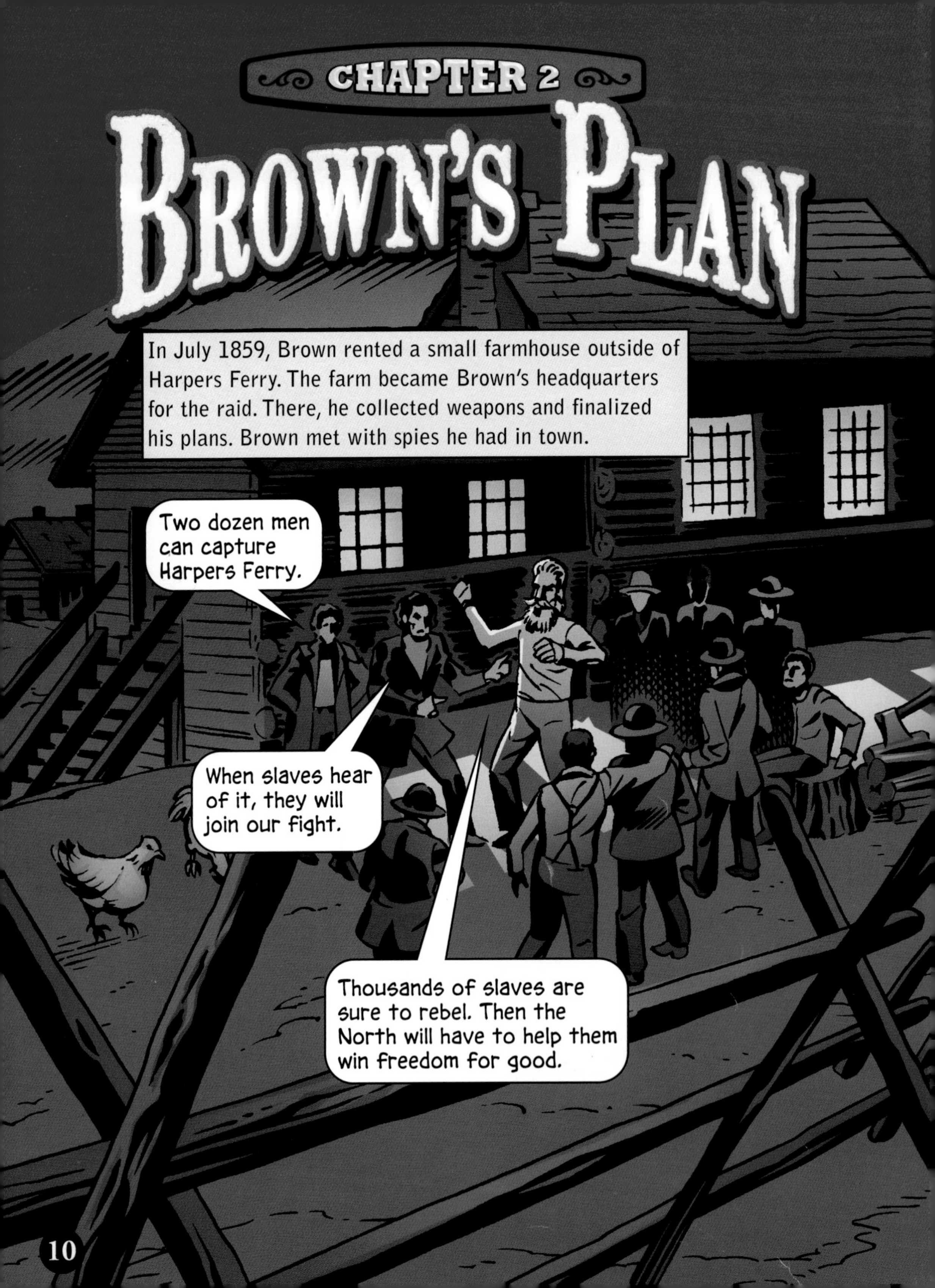
CHAPTER 2
BROWN'S PLAN
In July 1859, Brown rented a small farmhouse outside of Harpers Ferry. The farm became Brown's headquarters for the raid. There, he collected weapons and finalized his plans. Brown met with spies he had in town.
Two dozen men can capture Harpers Ferry.
When slaves hear of it, they will join our fight.
Thousands of slaves are sure to rebel. Then the North will have to help them win freedom for good.

For three days in August, Brown secretly met with a former slave named Frederick Douglass. Although Douglass was an abolitionist, he did not agree with Brown's plan.
Join me, old friend. With the town's weapons, we can lead the slaves to freedom.
You are going into a perfect steel trap.
Your plan will turn the country against all abolitionists.
Douglass did not join Brown but other black men did, including Dangerfield Newby. Newby was a free man, but his wife and children were slaves.
These weapons will win my family's freedom.

Brown expected more men to join him. But by September 1859, only 22 men had arrived.
My army is small but strong.
Brown couldn't wait for more men to arrive. He was afraid his plan would be discovered. His men were restless.
Father, we need to act soon. We are a small group, but we are yours.
I promise you, Owen, our actions will result in great things.
Brown also believed that thousands of slaves would hear of his attack and join his fight at Harpers Ferry.
Owen, when we leave for the Ferry, take these weapons to the schoolhouse near town.
The slaves will be well armed.

On the night of October 16, 1859, Brown decided to act. He gave his final orders for the raid.
Do not take the life of anyone, but if it is necessary, then make sure work of it.
Men, get on your arms. We will proceed to the Ferry.
Brown's men gathered their weapons and marched toward town.

CHAPTER 3
THE RAID

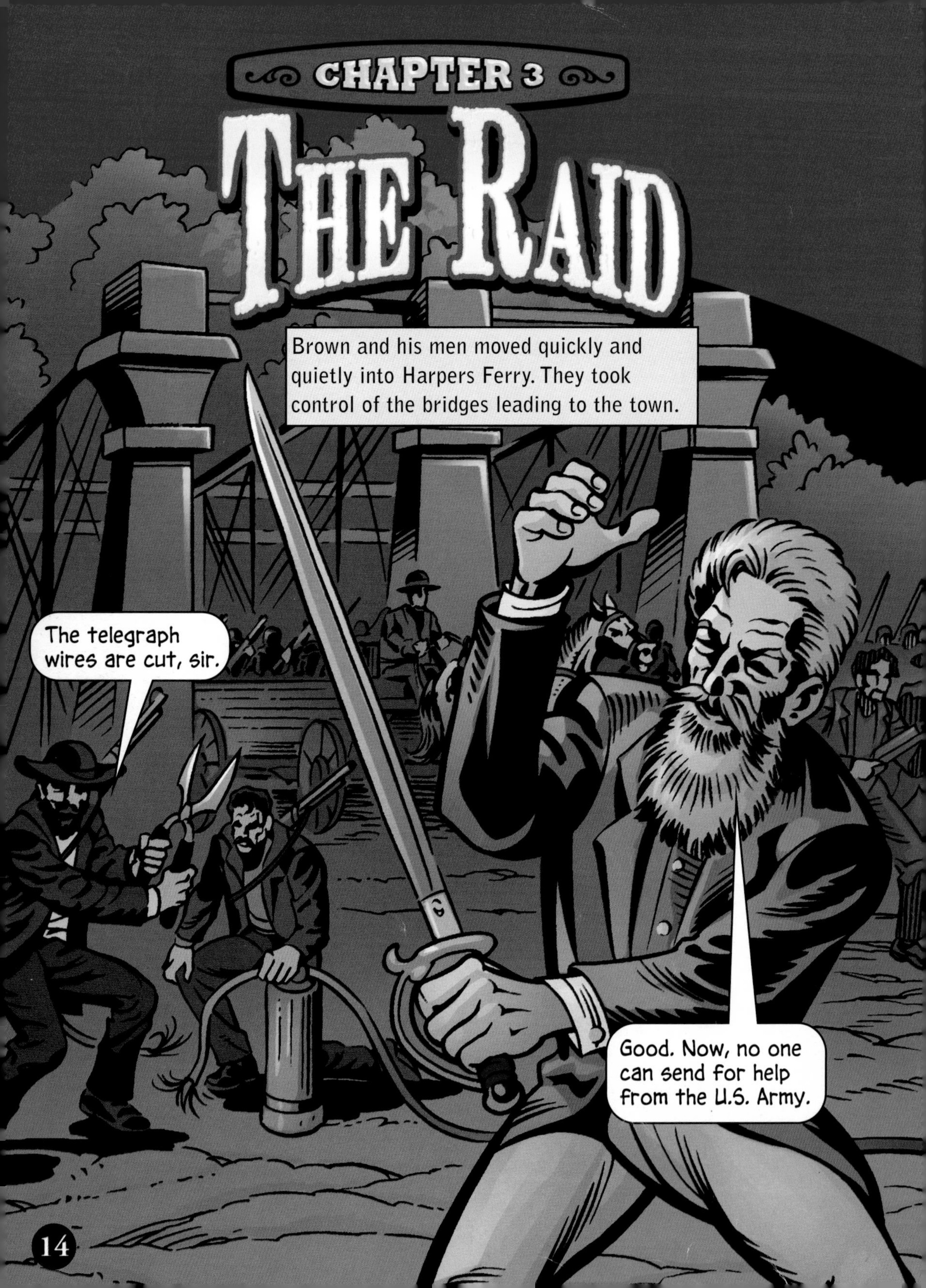

Brown and his men soon controlled the gates to the armory and arsenal. They took the guard prisoner.
I came here from Kansas, and this is a slave state. I want to free all the Negroes in this state.
Brown's plan changed when the guard escaped.
He's getting away!
STOP!
Brown said not to shoot unarmed men.
Brown hoped to capture Harpers Ferry while the townspeople were asleep. But the shots fired at the guard woke some of them.
That sounded like gunfire!

Word of Brown's raid began to spread through town. At 1:30 in the morning, a mail train reached Harpers Ferry. Brown wanted trains to pass by freely. He did not want word of his raid to reach other towns. The injured guard flagged down the train.
Madmen are taking the arsenal!
Hayward Shepherd was a free black man who worked for the railroad. Shepherd heard the guard say men were attacking. He went to see for himself.
The guard! He's coming back.
Stop! Hold your fire.
Brown's men thought Shepherd was the guard and shot him. Though badly wounded, Shepherd made it back to the train station.
Shepherd! What happened?
Help me. . .
The first person to die at Harpers Ferry was a free black man.

Brown's men quickly took control of the arsenal and armory. They held many townspeople prisoner.
The town is mine. Slaves will have their freedom.
Confident that his plan was working, Brown ordered the train to leave Harpers Ferry.
I don't need to kill innocent passengers. Now move your train.
Is this war?
Hurry! We need to warn others!
As the train sped out of town, the frightene passengers wrote notes about the attack. They threw the notes out the windows to warn people who might pass by the tracks.

At 7:05 that morning, U.S. President James Buchanan received news of Brown's raid.
Mr. President, Brown's raiders will be armed with the rifles from the arsenal.
Send Robert E. Lee and his troops to Harpers Ferry at once.
A group of soldiers from outside the city had also heard of the raid. They came to Harpers Ferry to defend the town. The militia charged up the street toward Brown and his men. Brown prepared for the attack.
Take aim, men.
Let go upon them.

The local militia was forced to retreat. But a few militiamen hid in buildings along the street. The two sides exchanged gunfire.
To the engine house! We must seek cover.
Someone has killed Newby!
As the hours passed, more people rushed to Harpers Ferry. They gathered weapons and joined the local militia. Brown's men were outnumbered and trapped.
Gather any weapon you can find!
This is how we treat murderers.

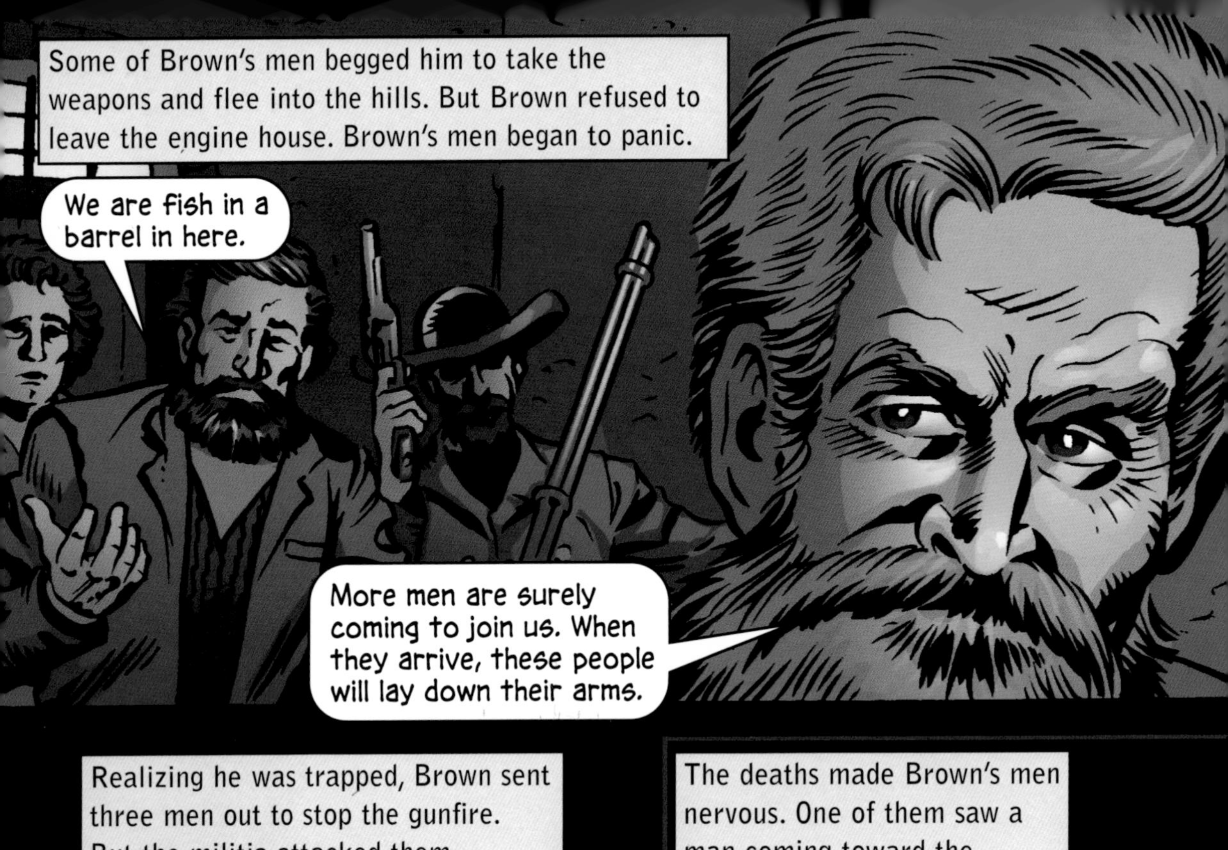
Some of Brown's men begged him to take the weapons and flee into the hills. But Brown refused to leave the engine house. Brown's men began to panic.
We are fish in a barrel in here.
More men are surely coming to join us. When they arrive, these people will lay down their arms.

Realizing he was trapped, Brown sent three men out to stop the gunfire. But the militia attacked them. Only Brown's son Watson returned. He was dying from a gunshot.
What kind of men are they, shooting down my men under a flag of truce?

The deaths made Brown's men nervous. One of them saw a man coming toward the engine house and shot him.
Brown's man had killed the Harpers Ferry mayor.

The mayor's death fueled the militia's anger. They searched the town for Brown's men. They captured and killed several of them. The militia then attacked the engine house again.
If help doesn't come soon, we're done for.
By now the slaves have heard of our attack. They are probably at the schoolhouse already.
Brown's son Owen had heard the gunfire from Harpers Ferry. He raced to the schoolhouse hoping to find thousands of men gathered.
No one was there.

On the morning of October 18, Lee and his troops arrived in Harpers Ferry. Lee sent a note to Brown asking him to surrender. Brown refused.
Storm the engine house.
Harder, men! Break down that door!
Brown and his men tried to block the door, but Lee's troops broke it down.

Lieutenant Israel Green was first inside.
He went straight for Brown. Brown fought back.
Now fire, men!
Green stabbed Brown with a light sword. The blade bent as it struck Brown. Green then beat Brown with the sword's handle.
Surrender!
Brown fell to the ground and was captured. After 36 hours, Brown's raid was over.
Some believed Brown was dead.
I think he's still alive!

CHAPTER 4
AFTER THE RAID
After his capture, government leaders visited Brown in jail. They questioned him about the raid.
Who helped you? Were abolitionists in the North behind this?
Why did you come here?
No man sent me here.
We came to free the slaves, and only that.

The state of Virginia charged Brown with treason, murder, and leading slaves to rebel.
RICHMOND WHIG
We find John Brown guilty of all charges.
Spare me the mockery of a public murder.
On November 2, 1859, Brown was sentenced to die by hanging.
Brown knew the fight over slavery was not finished. He never gave up calling for the freedom of slaves.
Charleston, Va. 2nd, December, 1859
I John Brown am now quite certain that
the crimes of this guilty, land: will never be
purged away but with Blood. I had as
I now think: vainly flattered
myself that without very much
bloodshed; it might be

Brown was hanged on December 2, 1859. Only soldiers were allowed to witness the hanging. Townspeople were afraid abolitionists might try to rescue Brown.
This man has divided the country.
I fear we are one step closer to war.
Many people saw John Brown as a hero. On the day of his death, slaves at nearby farms in Virginia set fire to their owner's buildings and poisoned some cattle.

One year after Brown's death, Southern states tried to form a new nation. They wanted to keep slavery legal. By 1861, the issue of slavery helped start the Civil War.

CHARGE!

Fire away, men!

Attack!

In his final note, Brown predicted that it would take "much bloodshed" to end slavery. At least 620,000 soldiers died during the Civil War. In 1865, the North won the war, and slavery in the South ended. That same year, the U.S. government passed the 13th Amendment to the Constitution, outlawing slavery forever.

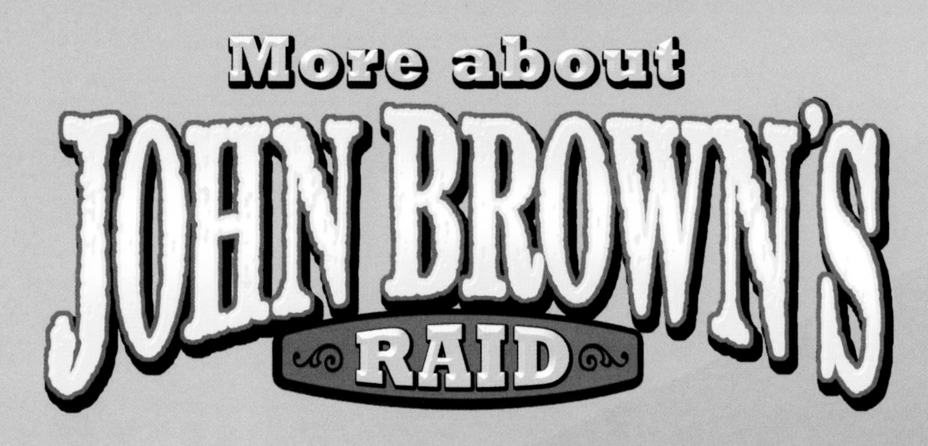

- John Brown was born May 9, 1800. He was 59 years old when he raided Harpers Ferry.
- Brown had 20 children. One son was killed in Kansas. Two sons died during the Harpers Ferry Raid.
- Secretary of War John B. Floyd received a letter in 1858 warning of Brown's plan to attack Harpers Ferry. Floyd didn't realize that Brown was the same man wanted for the Kansas murders. Floyd ignored the warning.
- Slaves did not join Brown's raid because few of them knew about his plans. Brown did not tell slaves at nearby plantations when he planned to raid Harpers Ferry.
- Many abolitionists supported Brown's plan. One group of rich and powerful supporters were later called the "Secret Six."

- Although Brown's plan was to free the slaves, two free black men were among the first to die in the Harpers Ferry raid.

- Sharps rifles were some of the best weapons available at the time. The capture of Brown and his 200 guns gave Virginia better weapons to use in the Civil War.

- Brown's trial lasted less than one week. The judge did not allow Brown to call any witnesses. The jury took less than one hour to find Brown guilty.

- During the Civil War, Northern soldiers sang a song with the words "John Brown's body lies a'mouldering in the grave. His truth is marching on." The tune for this song was later used for "The Battle Hymn of the Republic."

- A soldier named John Wilkes Booth attended Brown's hanging. In 1865, Booth shot and killed President Abraham Lincoln because he did not want Lincoln to end slavery.

GLOSSARY

armory (AR-mur-ee)—a place where weapons are stored

arsenal (AR-seh-null)—a large collection of weapons

consecrate (KOHN-se-krate)—to promise

militia (muh-LISH-uh)—a group of volunteer citizens who serve as soldiers in emergencies

telegraph (TEL-uh-graf)—a machine that uses electrical signals to send messages over long distances

treason (TREE-zuhn)—to betray one's country

truce (TROOS)—a temporary agreement to stop fighting

INTERNET SITES

FactHound offers a safe, fun way to find Internet sites related to this book. All of the sites on FactHound have been researched by our staff.

Here's how:

1. *Visit www.facthound.com*
2. Type in this special code **0736843698** for age-appropriate sites. Or enter a search word related to this book for a more general search.
3. Click on the **Fetch It** button.

FactHound will fetch the best sites for you!

READ MORE

De Capua, Sarah. *Abolitionists: A Force for Change.* Journey to Freedom. Chanhassen, Minn.: Child's World, 2003.

January, Brendan. *John Brown's Raid on Harpers Ferry.* Cornerstones of Freedom Series. Danbury, Conn.: Children's Press, 2000.

Lantier, Patricia. *Frederick Douglass.* Raintree Biographies. Austin, Texas: Raintree Steck-Vaughn, 2003.

McPherson, James M. *Fields of Fury: The American Civil War.* New York: Atheneum Books for Young Readers, 2002.

BIBLIOGRAPHY

Anderson, Osborne P. *A Voice From Harpers Ferry, 1859.* New York: World View Forum, 2000.

Douglass, Frederick. *Life and Times of Frederick Douglass.* Secaucus, N.J.: Citadel Press, 1983.

Oates, Stephen B. *To Purge This Land With Blood: A Biography of John Brown.* New York: Harper & Row, 1970.

Villard, Oswald Garrison. *John Brown, 1800-1859; a Biography Fifty Years After by Oswald Garrison Villard.* New York: Houghton Mifflin, 1910.

INDEX